Racism

Questions and Feelings About . . .

PICTURE WINDOW BOOKS
a capstone imprint

by Anita Ganeri
illustrated by Ximena Jeria

Questions and Feelings About . . . is published by
Picture Window Books, a Capstone imprint
1710 Roe Crest Drive, North Mankato, MN 56003
www.mycapstone.com

Library of Congress Cataloging-in-Publication Data is available on
the Library of Congress website.

ISBN: 978-1-5158-4542-3 (library binding)

Editor: Melanie Palmer
Design: Lisa Peacock
Author: Anita Ganeri

First published in Great Britain in 2018
by The Watts Publishing Group
Copyright © The Watts Publishing Group, 2018
All rights reserved.

Printed and bound in China.
001593

Racism

There are millions of people in the world.
Every one of us is different.

We look different. We wear different clothes. We speak different languages. We have different ways of living. We're good at different things.

What makes you different?

Even though we're all different, we're all human beings. We should value and respect everyone for who they are.

We should treat everyone fairly and equally.
Everyone should have the chance to live and
work together happily and peacefully.

*How would you like people
to treat you?*

Some people do not treat others fairly or equally. They treat them badly because they have different colored skin, come from different countries, speak differently, or wear different clothes.
This is called racism.
It is a kind of bullying.

Racism can mean saying unkind things to people. It can mean calling people names or making fun of the way they speak. It can mean teasing them about the way they look or dress.

How would you feel if someone called you names?

Racism can mean leaving someone out because they are different. It might mean not picking them for a game of soccer.

It might mean leaving them to sit on their
own at lunch.

*How would you feel
if you were left out?*

Racism can mean taking a person's things. It might mean stealing their money. It might mean ruining their belongings.

Racism can also mean hurting a person. The racists might push or shove them. They might hit them or trip them up.

Both children and adults can be racist.
Children may see or hear their parents
or other adults being racist and copy them.

But it doesn't matter who is being racist.
Racism is always wrong. It is never okay
for anyone to say or do racist things.

What makes you upset?

Racism makes people unhappy. It can make them feel unsafe and upset. It can make them scared to go to school or to leave their house.

Racism can make people feel ashamed of who they are, what they look like, and where they come from.

Why are some people racist? They may think that it's clever to be mean. They may think that they will be more popular if they say racist things.

It may be that they feel afraid of people who are different.

Often racists don't even know the person they are being mean to. They don't take time to find out anything about them.

They might think that people are strange because they wear different clothes. They do not understand that this is often a sign of their religion.

In some schools, children come from lots of different countries. Some left their homes because their lives were in danger. Some lost their families.

But other children may not take time getting to know them.

If someone is racist to you, don't keep it to yourself. Tell your parents, teacher, or another adult you trust.

Your parents or family could come into school to talk to your class. This could help other children understand things better.

Who would you tell?

27

Everyone is different, and that is a very good thing. Imagine how boring life would be if everyone was exactly the same!

We can learn a lot from each other. We can learn about different countries, different religions, and different ways of life. We can learn to live together peacefully and happily.

Notes for Caregivers

This book can be a useful way for families and professionals to begin a discussion with children about aspects of racism and discrimination. Racism can happen in all walks of life and has a devastating impact on its victims. In an increasingly multicultural society, it is vital that children learn to tolerate and respect others and value differences.

Speaking out about racism can be very daunting and takes a great deal of courage. Racism is a form of bullying. Victims are often intimidated by the bullies and afraid to speak out. By identifying someone they can trust and talk to safely (an adult, friend, or an organization), children can take the first step to being listened to and finding help.

Emphasising the need for respect and tolerance of others can help tackle racist attitudes before they become entrenched. Likewise, a discussion of difference and diversity can help children understand and accept that we are not all the same and should be valued for the unique human beings that we are.

Group Activities

1. Get the group to think about what it feels like to be discriminated against. For example, treat some of the children (perhaps those with brown hair or brown eyes) more favorably than the others. How do the other children feel? Is it fair that they are treated less favorably because their hair or eyes are a different color?

2. Ask the children what they would do if they saw or heard someone being racist. Talk about what they would do. Would they keep calm and walk away? Would they tell someone? If so, who? Talk about how the school has strict rules about racism.

3. Get the group to think about their own families and draw a family tree, showing where different family members were born and where they live. This may help show that most of us have relatives who come from all over the world.

4. Ignorance is often at the root of racism. Invite a parent or caregiver to talk about their culture and religion so that misunderstandings can be avoided. Have the children prepare questions to ask.

Read More:

Lacey, Jane. *Dealing with Racism*. Powerkids Press, 2019.

Raphael, Mayma. *I Love the Skin I'm In!* Mom Publishing, 2012.

Spilsbury, Louise. *Racism and Intolerance*. B.E.S. Publishing, 2018.

Read the entire Questions and Feelings About . . . series:
Adoption
Autism
Bullying
Having a Disability
Racism
When Parents Separate
When Someone Dies
Worries